Dream Journal

Date:_______________   Time:_______________

Thoughts Before Sleep

Emotions Before Sleep

Dream

Interpretation

Feeling Upon Awakening

Comments

Dream Journal

Date:_____________   Time:_____________

Thoughts Before Sleep

____

____

____

____

Emotions Before Sleep

____

Dream

____

____

____

____

____

____

____

Interpretation

____

____

____

Feeling Upon Awakening

____

____

____

____

Comments

____

____

____

Dream Journal

Date:_____________   Time:_____________

Thoughts Before Sleep

Emotions Before Sleep

Dream

Interpretation

Feeling Upon Awakening

Comments

Dream Journal

Date:_____________   Time:_____________

Thoughts Before Sleep

Emotions Before Sleep

Dream

Interpretation

Feeling Upon Awakening

Comments

Dream Journal

Date:_____________   Time:_____________

Thoughts Before Sleep

Emotions Before Sleep

Dream

Interpretation

Feeling Upon Awakening

Comments

Dream Journal

Date:____________   Time:____________

Thoughts Before Sleep

Emotions Before Sleep

Dream

Interpretation

Feeling Upon Awakening

Comments

Dream Journal

Date:______________   Time:______________

Thoughts Before Sleep

Emotions Before Sleep

Dream

Interpretation

Feeling Upon Awakening

Comments

Dream Journal

Date:_______________   Time:_______________

Thoughts Before Sleep

____

____

____

____

____

Emotions Before Sleep

____

Dream

____

____

____

____

____

____

____

____

Interpretation

____

____

____

Feeling Upon Awakening

____

____

____

Comments

____

____

____

Dream Journal

Date:_______________   Time:_______________

Thoughts Before Sleep

Emotions Before Sleep

Dream

Interpretation

Feeling Upon Awakening

Comments

Dream Journal

Date:______________   Time:______________

Thoughts Before Sleep

Emotions Before Sleep

Dream

Interpretation

Feeling Upon Awakening

Comments

Dream Journal

Date:______________   Time:______________

Thoughts Before Sleep

Emotions Before Sleep

Dream

Interpretation

Feeling Upon Awakening

Comments

Dream Journal

Date:___________   Time:___________

Thoughts Before Sleep

Emotions Before Sleep

Dream

Interpretation

Feeling Upon Awakening

Comments

Dream Journal

Date:_______________   Time:_______________

Thoughts Before Sleep

Emotions Before Sleep

Dream

Interpretation

Feeling Upon Awakening

Comments

Dream Journal

Date:____________   Time:____________

Thoughts Before Sleep

____

____

____

____

____

Emotions Before Sleep

____

Dream

____

____

____

____

____

____

____

Interpretation

____

____

____

Feeling Upon Awakening

____

____

____

Comments

____

____

____

Dream Journal

Date:___________   Time:___________

Thoughts Before Sleep

Emotions Before Sleep

Dream

Interpretation

Feeling Upon Awakening

Comments

Dream Journal

Date:______________   Time:______________

Thoughts Before Sleep

Emotions Before Sleep

Dream

Interpretation

Feeling Upon Awakening

Comments

Dream Journal

Date:_____________   Time:___________

Thoughts Before Sleep

Emotions Before Sleep

Dream

Interpretation

Feeling Upon Awakening

Comments

Dream Journal

Date:_______________   Time:_____________

Thoughts Before Sleep

Emotions Before Sleep

Dream

Interpretation

Feeling Upon Awakening

Comments

Dream Journal

Date:_______________   Time:_____________

Thoughts Before Sleep

Emotions Before Sleep

Dream

Interpretation

Feeling Upon Awakening

Comments

Dream Journal

Date:_____________   Time:_____________

Thoughts Before Sleep

____

____

____

____

Emotions Before Sleep

____

Dream

____

____

____

____

____

____

____

Interpretation

____

____

____

Feeling Upon Awakening

____

____

____

Comments

____

____

Dream Journal

Date:____________   Time:____________

Thoughts Before Sleep

Emotions Before Sleep

Dream

Interpretation

Feeling Upon Awakening

Comments

Dream Journal

Date:_____________   Time:_____________

Thoughts Before Sleep

Emotions Before Sleep

Dream

Interpretation

Feeling Upon Awakening

Comments

Dream Journal

Date:__________________   Time:__________________

Thoughts Before Sleep

Emotions Before Sleep

Dream

Interpretation

Feeling Upon Awakening

Comments

Dream Journal

Date:_______________   Time:______________

Thoughts Before Sleep

Emotions Before Sleep

Dream

Interpretation

Feeling Upon Awakening

Comments

Dream Journal

Date:_____________   Time:_____________

Thoughts Before Sleep

Emotions Before Sleep

Dream

Interpretation

Feeling Upon Awakening

Comments

Dream Journal

Date:_____________   Time:_____________

Thoughts Before Sleep

Emotions Before Sleep

Dream

Interpretation

Feeling Upon Awakening

Comments

Dream Journal

Date:_______________   Time:_______________

Thoughts Before Sleep

Emotions Before Sleep

Dream

Interpretation

Feeling Upon Awakening

Comments

Dream Journal

Date:______________   Time:______________

Thoughts Before Sleep

Emotions Before Sleep

Dream

Interpretation

Feeling Upon Awakening

Comments

Dream Journal

Date:_____________   Time:_____________

Thoughts Before Sleep

Emotions Before Sleep

Dream

Interpretation

Feeling Upon Awakening

Comments

Dream Journal

Date:_____________   Time:_____________

Thoughts Before Sleep

Emotions Before Sleep

Dream

Interpretation

Feeling Upon Awakening

Comments

Dream Journal

Date:_____________   Time:_____________

Thoughts Before Sleep

Emotions Before Sleep

Dream

Interpretation

Feeling Upon Awakening

Comments

Dream Journal

Date:_______________   Time:_______________

Thoughts Before Sleep

Emotions Before Sleep

Dream

Interpretation

Feeling Upon Awakening

Comments

Dream Journal

Date:______________   Time:______________

Thoughts Before Sleep

Emotions Before Sleep

Dream

Interpretation

Feeling Upon Awakening

Comments

Dream Journal

Date:_____________   Time:_____________

Thoughts Before Sleep

Emotions Before Sleep

Dream

Interpretation

Feeling Upon Awakening

Comments

Dream Journal

Date:_______________ Time:_____________

Thoughts Before Sleep

Emotions Before Sleep

Dream

Interpretation

Feeling Upon Awakening

Comments

Dream Journal

Date:___________   Time:___________

Thoughts Before Sleep

Emotions Before Sleep

Dream

Interpretation

Feeling Upon Awakening

Comments

Dream Journal

Date:______________   Time:______________

Thoughts Before Sleep

Emotions Before Sleep

Dream

Interpretation

Feeling Upon Awakening

Comments

Dream Journal

Date:___________________   Time:___________________

Thoughts Before Sleep

Emotions Before Sleep

Dream

Interpretation

Feeling Upon Awakening

Comments

Dream Journal

Date:_____________ Time:_____________

Thoughts Before Sleep

Emotions Before Sleep

Dream

Interpretation

Feeling Upon Awakening

Comments

Dream Journal

Date:_______________   Time:_______________

Thoughts Before Sleep

Emotions Before Sleep

Dream

Interpretation

Feeling Upon Awakening

Comments

Dream Journal

Date:___________   Time:___________

Thoughts Before Sleep

Emotions Before Sleep

Dream

Interpretation

Feeling Upon Awakening

Comments

Dream Journal

Date:_____________   Time:___________

Thoughts Before Sleep

Emotions Before Sleep

Dream

Interpretation

Feeling Upon Awakening

Comments

Dream Journal

Date:___________   Time:___________

Thoughts Before Sleep

Emotions Before Sleep

Dream

Interpretation

Feeling Upon Awakening

Comments

Dream Journal

Date:_____________   Time:_____________

Thoughts Before Sleep

____

____

____

____

____

Emotions Before Sleep

____

Dream

____

____

____

____

____

____

____

____

____

Interpretation

____

____

____

Feeling Upon Awakening

____

____

____

Comments

____

____

____

Dream Journal

Date:_______________   Time:_______________

Thoughts Before Sleep

Emotions Before Sleep

Dream

Interpretation

Feeling Upon Awakening

Comments

Dream Journal

Date:_____________   Time:____________

Thoughts Before Sleep

Emotions Before Sleep

Dream

Interpretation

Feeling Upon Awakening

Comments

Dream Journal

Date:_____________   Time:_____________

Thoughts Before Sleep

Emotions Before Sleep

Dream

Interpretation

Feeling Upon Awakening

Comments

Dream Journal

Date:______________   Time:______________

Thoughts Before Sleep

Emotions Before Sleep

Dream

Interpretation

Feeling Upon Awakening

Comments

Dream Journal

Date:______________   Time:______________

Thoughts Before Sleep

Emotions Before Sleep

Dream

Interpretation

Feeling Upon Awakening

Comments

Dream Journal

Date:____________   Time:____________

Thoughts Before Sleep

____

____

____

____

____

Emotions Before Sleep

____

Dream

____

____

____

____

____

____

____

Interpretation

____

____

____

Feeling Upon Awakening

____

____

____

____

Comments

____

____

____

Dream Journal

Date:_____________   Time:_____________

Thoughts Before Sleep

Emotions Before Sleep

Dream

Interpretation

Feeling Upon Awakening

Comments

Dream Journal

Date:_______________   Time:_____________

Thoughts Before Sleep

Emotions Before Sleep

Dream

Interpretation

Feeling Upon Awakening

Comments

Dream Journal

Date:______________   Time:____________

Thoughts Before Sleep

Emotions Before Sleep

Dream

Interpretation

Feeling Upon Awakening

Comments

Dream Journal

Date:_______________   Time:______________

Thoughts Before Sleep

Emotions Before Sleep

Dream

Interpretation

Feeling Upon Awakening

Comments

Dream Journal

Date:_____________   Time:_____________

Thoughts Before Sleep

Emotions Before Sleep

Dream

Interpretation

Feeling Upon Awakening

Comments

Dream Journal

Date:_____________   Time:___________

Thoughts Before Sleep

Emotions Before Sleep

Dream

Interpretation

Feeling Upon Awakening

Comments

Dream Journal

Date:_____________   Time:___________

Thoughts Before Sleep

Emotions Before Sleep

Dream

Interpretation

Feeling Upon Awakening

Comments

Dream Journal

Date:______________   Time:______________

Thoughts Before Sleep

Emotions Before Sleep

Dream

Interpretation

Feeling Upon Awakening

Comments

Dream Journal

Date:_______________   Time:____________

Thoughts Before Sleep

Emotions Before Sleep

Dream

Interpretation

Feeling Upon Awakening

Comments

Dream Journal

Date:________________   Time:____________

Thoughts Before Sleep

Emotions Before Sleep

Dream

Interpretation

Feeling Upon Awakening

Comments

Dream Journal

Date:_____________   Time:_____________

Thoughts Before Sleep

Emotions Before Sleep

Dream

Interpretation

Feeling Upon Awakening

Comments

Dream Journal

Date:______________   Time:______________

Thoughts Before Sleep

____

____

____

____

Emotions Before Sleep

____

Dream

____

____

____

____

____

____

____

Interpretation

____

____

____

Feeling Upon Awakening

____

____

____

____

Comments

____

____

____

Dream Journal

Date:______________ Time:______________

Thoughts Before Sleep

Emotions Before Sleep

Dream

Interpretation

Feeling Upon Awakening

Comments

Dream Journal

Date:_____________   Time:_____________

Thoughts Before Sleep

Emotions Before Sleep

Dream

Interpretation

Feeling Upon Awakening

Comments

Dream Journal

Date:___________________   Time:_______________

Thoughts Before Sleep

Emotions Before Sleep

Dream

Interpretation

Feeling Upon Awakening

Comments

Dream Journal

Date:____________   Time:____________

Thoughts Before Sleep

Emotions Before Sleep

Dream

Interpretation

Feeling Upon Awakening

Comments

Dream Journal

Date:_____________   Time:_____________

Thoughts Before Sleep

Emotions Before Sleep

Dream

Interpretation

Feeling Upon Awakening

Comments

Dream Journal

Date:_____________   Time:_____________

Thoughts Before Sleep

Emotions Before Sleep

Dream

Interpretation

Feeling Upon Awakening

Comments

Dream Journal

Date:_____________   Time:_____________

Thoughts Before Sleep

Emotions Before Sleep

Dream

Interpretation

Feeling Upon Awakening

Comments

Dream Journal

Date:_____________   Time:_____________

Thoughts Before Sleep

Emotions Before Sleep

Dream

Interpretation

Feeling Upon Awakening

Comments

Dream Journal

Date:_______________   Time:___________

Thoughts Before Sleep

Emotions Before Sleep

Dream

Interpretation

Feeling Upon Awakening

Comments

Dream Journal

Date:______________ Time:______________

Thoughts Before Sleep

Emotions Before Sleep

Dream

Interpretation

Feeling Upon Awakening

Comments

Dream Journal

Date:_______________   Time:_______________

Thoughts Before Sleep

Emotions Before Sleep

Dream

Interpretation

Feeling Upon Awakening

Comments

Dream Journal

Date:_____________   Time:_____________

Thoughts Before Sleep

____

____

____

____

Emotions Before Sleep

____

Dream

____

____

____

____

____

____

____

Interpretation

____

____

____

Feeling Upon Awakening

____

____

____

____

Comments

____

____

____

Dream Journal

Date:______________   Time:____________

Thoughts Before Sleep

Emotions Before Sleep

Dream

Interpretation

Feeling Upon Awakening

Comments

Dream Journal

Date:____________________   Time:____________________

Thoughts Before Sleep

Emotions Before Sleep

Dream

Interpretation

Feeling Upon Awakening

Comments

Dream Journal

Date:_____________   Time:_____________

Thoughts Before Sleep

Emotions Before Sleep

Dream

Interpretation

Feeling Upon Awakening

Comments

Dream Journal

Date:_____________   Time:___________

Thoughts Before Sleep

Emotions Before Sleep

Dream

Interpretation

Feeling Upon Awakening

Comments

Dream Journal

Date:______________   Time:______________

Thoughts Before Sleep

Emotions Before Sleep

Dream

Interpretation

Feeling Upon Awakening

Comments

Dream Journal

Date:___________   Time:___________

Thoughts Before Sleep

Emotions Before Sleep

Dream

Interpretation

Feeling Upon Awakening

Comments

Dream Journal

Date:______________   Time:______________

Thoughts Before Sleep

Emotions Before Sleep

Dream

Interpretation

Feeling Upon Awakening

Comments

Dream Journal

Date:_____________   Time:_____________

Thoughts Before Sleep

Emotions Before Sleep

Dream

Interpretation

Feeling Upon Awakening

Comments

Dream Journal

Date:_____________   Time:_____________

Thoughts Before Sleep

Emotions Before Sleep

Dream

Interpretation

Feeling Upon Awakening

Comments

Dream Journal

Date:_______________   Time:_______________

Thoughts Before Sleep

____

____

____

____

Emotions Before Sleep

____

Dream

____

____

____

____

____

____

____

Interpretation

____

____

____

Feeling Upon Awakening

____

____

____

____

Comments

____

____

____

Dream Journal

Date:___________   Time:___________

Thoughts Before Sleep

Emotions Before Sleep

Dream

Interpretation

Feeling Upon Awakening

Comments

Dream Journal

Date:_____________   Time:____________

Thoughts Before Sleep

____

____

____

____

Emotions Before Sleep

____

Dream

____

____

____

____

____

____

____

Interpretation

____

____

____

Feeling Upon Awakening

____

____

____

Comments

____

____

____

Dream Journal

Date:_____________   Time:_____________

Thoughts Before Sleep

Emotions Before Sleep

Dream

Interpretation

Feeling Upon Awakening

Comments

Dream Journal

Date:____________   Time:____________

Thoughts Before Sleep

Emotions Before Sleep

Dream

Interpretation

Feeling Upon Awakening

Comments

Dream Journal

Date:_____________   Time:___________

Thoughts Before Sleep

Emotions Before Sleep

Dream

Interpretation

Feeling Upon Awakening

Comments

Dream Journal

Date:____________   Time:____________

Thoughts Before Sleep

Emotions Before Sleep

Dream

Interpretation

Feeling Upon Awakening

Comments

Dream Journal

Date:_____________   Time:_____________

Thoughts Before Sleep

Emotions Before Sleep

Dream

Interpretation

Feeling Upon Awakening

Comments

Dream Journal

Date:___________________   Time:___________________

Thoughts Before Sleep

____

____

____

____

____

Emotions Before Sleep

____

Dream

____

____

____

____

____

____

____

____

Interpretation

____

____

____

Feeling Upon Awakening

____

____

____

____

Comments

____

____

____

Dream Journal

Date:______________   Time:____________

Thoughts Before Sleep

Emotions Before Sleep

Dream

Interpretation

Feeling Upon Awakening

Comments

Dream Journal

Date:_____________   Time:_____________

Thoughts Before Sleep

Emotions Before Sleep

Dream

Interpretation

Feeling Upon Awakening

Comments

Dream Journal

Date:___________   Time:___________

Thoughts Before Sleep

Emotions Before Sleep

Dream

Interpretation

Feeling Upon Awakening

Comments

Dream Journal

Date:_____________   Time:_____________

Thoughts Before Sleep

____

____

____

____

Emotions Before Sleep

____

Dream

____

____

____

____

____

____

____

Interpretation

____

____

____

Feeling Upon Awakening

____

____

____

Comments

____

____

____

Dream Journal

Date:______________   Time:______________

Thoughts Before Sleep

Emotions Before Sleep

Dream

Interpretation

Feeling Upon Awakening

Comments

Dream Journal

Date:______________   Time:______________

Thoughts Before Sleep

____

____

____

____

Emotions Before Sleep

____

Dream

____

____

____

____

____

____

____

Interpretation

____

____

Feeling Upon Awakening

____

____

____

Comments

____

____

____

Dream Journal

Date:____________ Time:____________

Thoughts Before Sleep

Emotions Before Sleep

Dream

Interpretation

Feeling Upon Awakening

Comments

Dream Journal

Date:____________ Time:____________

Thoughts Before Sleep

Emotions Before Sleep

Dream

Interpretation

Feeling Upon Awakening

Comments

www.ingramcontent.com/pod-product-compliance
Lightning Source LLC
Chambersburg PA
CBHW051443150726
48000CB00005B/2222